Then, Now

Poems 1971-2016

Jeffrey A. Del Col

Then, Now
Poems 1971-2016

by Jeffrey A. Del Col

Cover photograph by Jeffrey A. Del Col

Cover and interior design by Rob Reaser

ISBN: 978-1986666701

Published by Jumping Spider Press

Jeffrey A. Del Col

Jeffrey A. Del Col earned undergraduate and graduate degrees in English from West Virginia University and a doctorate in technology education, also from West Virginia University. He taught English for two years at Glenville State College in West Virginia and then for 37 years taught composition, creative writing, literature, humanities, and honors courses at Alderson-Broaddus College (now Alderson Broaddus University) in Philippi, West Virginia. He was a cofounder of and faculty advisor to the Alderson Broaddus literary publication, *InFlux*, and served for several years as editor of *Grab-a-Nickel*, a nationally circulated publication of the Barbour County Writers' Workshop.

He was an avid reader and scholar with widely diverse interests, many of which are reflected in his poetry. In addition to his scholarly pursuits, he was a flower gardener, raising an impressive array of cacti, orchids, roses, and other flowering plants; and a dedicated birdwatcher with an impressive knowledge of the birds of West Virginia, Florida, the United Kingdom, and elsewhere.

He died in 2016 before he could complete assembling this collection, but it was completed by his wife, Carol Del Col, and arranged by Carol and their daughter, Laura Del Col Brown.

Introduction

This collection opens on a note of bittersweet synchronicity. "Memento Mori" was one of my father's last published poems. Inspired by Shostakovich's Sonata for Viola and Piano, it was accepted by an obscure publication devoted to the composer, the *DSCH Journal*, at around the same time as my own poem "Opus 6," which is about Shostakovich's early Suite for Two Pianos. Neither of us had known the other was working on a poem about Shostakovich, although we both had a deep love of his music. But the link between the two pieces was stronger than that, for the Viola Sonata quotes directly from the Suite. Shostakovich wrote the Suite shortly after his father's unexpected death, and dedicated it to his memory; the Sonata was his final completed work, written when he knew he himself was dying.

The coincidence—startling, melancholy, rooted in art—is a fitting introduction to my father's work, where we repeatedly find the mystical embedded in the ordinary. The topic of mortality is never far from these poems, although there's a sense that death is just a way-station on the journey into history. In "Alla Danza Tedesca," one of Beethoven's final string quartets (which, like Shostakovich's Viola Sonata, was not performed till after the composer's death) is punctuated by a vision of my grandparents engaged in a defiant peasant dance "before the tide of sleep and forgetting." To be "forgotten by those who did and did not know" ("The Twilight of the Gods") is the only real death; as the title poem of this collection observes, love and memory "defy time and space, at least for now."

Two concepts appear again and again in my father's writings— not just his poems, but his class lectures and even his Facebook posts. They are evil and grace. "Evil" was a term he used frequently but not lightly; his conception of it was strongly influenced by Joseph Brodsky, who, in his commencement address to Williams

College in 1984, described it as "capable of a fairly ubiquitous presence if only because it tends to appear in the guise of good," and advised his hearers that "the surest defence against Evil is extreme individualism, originality of thinking, whimsicality, even— if you will—eccentricity." (Brodsky, by the way, was one of many oppressed writers my father sympathised with and campaigned for; "Palimpsests" is inspired directly by the story of the Soviet poet Irina Ratushinskaya, who carved her poems into bars of prison soap with matchsticks.)

And grace? It could be found everywhere, in the beauty of nature ("Sandhill Crane," "Anglewings"), the transcendence of art ("Vermeer—The Art of Painting") or in "simple moments" of everyday kindness ("Ministers of Grace"). My father had no particular personal faith, despite his on-again, off-again relationship with the Catholic Church that he was born into; but he never abandoned the idea of another dimension that lay behind and enhanced the everyday. As he writes in "Pleasant Creek, December":

> Surmounting the dark wind
> the call of the earth,
> not spirit, but presence,
> persists,
> against the reeds, the ducks, the dark water,
> the day itself.

— Laura Del Col Brown

Contents

Memento Mori

(Shostakovich's Sonata for Piano and Viola, op. 147)

Twelve tones resolve to stranger harmonies,
bitter history of smoke and blood,
chaos of time's divisions,
a heart's guttering rhythm.

A fool's caper,
salto mortale,
terrified scherzo of skeletal fingers
prankish with moonlight.

A disc of bone, low and white,
bleached stone bright on the rim of Moscow hills.
Moonlight echoed,
plangent on piano and viola,
a tribute to that most difficult deaf man,
a farewell washed clean by moonlight
unpassionate now,
unfettered by mortality.

The Goldfinch

Sullen harlequin,
No byzantine lord to amuse
With what is, or was, or will be news.
But tethered on a chain of brass
For pillars of the middle class,
And heaven's rage goes unfelt,
Around the burgher's house in Delft.
Where Carel Fabritius limned the finch,
Red, and gold, and white, and black
Upon its perch, upon its rack.

The Devil at Isenheim

Summoned to view a rude and ordinary birth,
he looks puzzled,
cloaked in gangrenous feathers,
capped with a peacock's crest,
forced to finger the frets of a ruined viol,
to harmonize with the Host he so detests.
Elsewhere his minions annoy Saint Anthony,
and the main attraction, a thoroughly dead Savior,
is quite to his taste.
But that risen radiance in the other frame,
—not the saintly, no doubt boring, chat
of Paul the Hermit and Anthony in an imagined wilderness,
nor the pious fraud of the Annunciation.
No, that other frame, the Son rising,
dazzling the guards with blinding humility,
where did that come from?
Does He really expect him to believe
that the pudgy, somewhat elderly infant
dandled by His infuriatingly pure mother
could pull something like that three decades later?

Vermeer—*The Art of Painting*

While the portrait of the artist toils away
in slashed doublet and rakish hat,
Clio stands bemused or bored,
tired of impersonation.
No pearls, rakes or virginals,
just laurels, a book, a trombone,
a map, some scattered papers,
accoutrements of allegory artfully arrayed,
bait for critics
and endless wrangles about technique,
or accusations of fraud via camera obscura,
blind to another reading,
to perception changed to impulse,
to color, shape and line,
another transubstantiation.

Clio's Mirror

To humor the classical tradition
which made her keeper of glory
and the winners' reputations,
History, if Vermeer can be trusted,
posed with laurel crowns,
trumpets and books of praise.
But carefully hidden from the painter's sight,
kept her real badge of office,
a kaleidoscope of sticks and stones,
old bones,
old news, old fears,
salt crystals of dead tears,
ink and soot, and laurel leaves,
tell-tales of blood, and lives bereaved
informed by reflection,
mutation and correction.

Icon Russe

A single ambiguous gout of red
carries Elijah heavenward,
old covenant and new,
prophet, horses and chariot,
in a scarlet amphiboly,
a double baptism,
cleansing fire,
precious blood.

Bosch's *The Last Judgment*

It was downhill from the start,
Eve, the Serpent,
a parrot-winged angel with sword.

Life—was a pinakothek of torment.
Pierced, racked, scorched, crushed;
you name it,
we deserved it.

After that—Hell.

—or a very small Heaven,
few saints, no excitement.

Printer's Devil

"I'll burn my books!" cried Faust, too late,
blaming perdition on print.
He had a point—
the honey drop at the top of the slate
might well mask poison,
until, like Mithridates, we die old,
but nevertheless,
bitten by acedia's black bitch,
until sly necromancy
of words, words, words,
pitches us toward the abyss,
playthings for the winking, smirking,
urgent jester at reason's funeral.

Palimpsests

It does no good to jail them,
the poets,
the graphomanic tribe,
the people of the book.

No good at all.

It doesn't cure them of what troubles you.

They do it anyway.

With dirt or chalk or blood,
Scrawled into the dust or slime
On cement walls or floors.

Or carved with burnt ends of matches on bars of soap
When they should be cleansing themselves
Instead of making things rough for whoever washes next.

Guidelines for Book Longevity

The enemies of books are many.
They must outlast
fire,
water,
mold,
bookworms,
(invertebrate or not)
censors and other vermin,
persist, like drooped timepieces,
their pages proof
against oxidation's glacial fire,
erosion by ignorance,
or pedagogical insolence.

Girl at Twelve

The iron chair angles newborn curves,
just begun to bloom
around the linear frankness of the child.
Eyes unschooled in guile,
knotted brows, sullen lip,
a quip or snarl withheld
for some unpublic place
away from the camera's chase
for truth in time's scheme
to trip her out of childhood.

Back Seat Dodge '38

Eddie Kienholz built a car,
a staticmobile, no wheels,
a foreshortened dream machine
flocked in nightmare blue velvet.
Backseat only behind the grille,
the bare essentials laid bare
to any voyeur of backseat action,
where, presumably fueled by four beers,
two mannequins meld amid machinery,
one plaster, one chicken wire,
legs. torsos, one privately intruding hand,
right next to Barney's Beanery.

Chrome Nude

Immaculata of the mudflaps,
Tantric icon of the roads,
Posture of promise,
Impostor of desire,

Our lady of the highways,
Pose for us sinners.
Grant us what mercy metal allows.

Safe from yielding to a sigh,
Return our desire,
Untarnished daughter of Eve,
Icy outline of concupiscence.

Bassoon buffoonery

Cartoon lunacy,
A goon show
Apes tricked out in green galloons
(or should be, such baboonery)
Moon mad at high noon,
Minus bouzouki…and didgeridoo.

Pleasant Creek, December

At year's end dry reeds shuffle,
stirring dark water smudged with ice.
Ducks wheel and gabble
against a tumult of gray and blue.
A raven harries a marsh hawk
above snow and stubble.
Surmounting the dark wind
the call of the earth,
not spirit, but presence,
persists,
against the reeds, the ducks, the dark water,
the day itself.

Sandhill Crane

The great bird drifted,
far above remnant Florida scrub,
wings stretched below bands of cloud,
ever slowly southward,
riding the warm rush of upward air.
But for that southward easing,
it bent no wing to rise or fall,
made no raucous, clattering cry
inviting or warning other cranes.
Mute and solitary, defying its nature,
as near transcendence as flesh allows,
or so an observer might think,
standing in the slow, narcotic heat,
stunned by an epiphany of his own making.

Aloft

In a sky bright enough for Vermeer,
flutters of color too high for leaves
straggle across skeins of cirrus.

Monarchs or Painted Ladies,
in disciplined drift past the edge of equinox,
and autumn's counterfeit copper and gold.

Mutability on the wind,
pursuing milkweed and thistle
beyond summer's horizon.

Aristophanic

Beneath a March sky clean of clouds,
a chorus, loud
through bare trees
a querulous gabble
persistent on the warm edged breeze,
scores of ducks in colloquy, it seemed,
until sight denied hearing
—two wood ducks, one mallard—
but myriad wood frogs and peepers
koax-ing, squeaking
amphibian uproar
lacking only Aeschylus,
aboard a skiff,
returned from Hades by popular demand.

The Chrysalis

Dark husk on dead stem
simple evidence of renaissance,
no parade of maudlin omen,
no unastonished angel.

Wings scaled with bright dust
lift transfigured flesh aloft,
to search for sugar, salt and minerals
at gaudy nectar, dung heap,
and muddy seep,
or sweaty brows in search of epiphanies.

Winter Haiku

Pregnant does paw snow
Finding frozen maple leaves;
Winter starving spring.

Crows perch in bare trees
Caucusing among themselves;
Black cloaks shedding snow.

In urgent tumult
Three foxes enflame the snow;
One suitor returns.

Wildlife

An enclave of aliens
practice sensual mimicry,
adopt postures of desire,
perfume the air with violets and vanilla,
mothballs and the occasional dead rat,
for hymenopterans half a world away,
or long-tongued moths
or carrion flies.

Early Ripe

Apricots flower before
the tide of winter recedes.
Tricked by memory of the Levant,
limbs ladder with flowers,
fragile tissue, self-betrayed.
June's dusky amber fruit
gone with April's frost.

Winterkill

A wasp born too soon for spring
starves on a veined sill,
on a new leaf of a rose
fostered through winter on the marble ledge.

A thin gold ring bisects its waist
below ovals of dusky rose,
the sleek mechanical tilts
the brutal wedge of its head,
scans the sky beyond the glass.

On blades of buzzing smoky quartz
it moves up the pane
tapping,
turreting,
in spendthrift frenzy
matching cold experience
against rules engraved
on fast cooling nerves.

Initiated

Starlings, too loud, too bold,
despised invaders of native space,
clean their beaks after feasting—
as do parrots,
much loved despite their shrieking.
Starlings, too numerous, too rude,
preen their spangled plumes,
snare flakes of sunlight
to belie their drabness,
no argus-eyed clichés of pride and the devil,
but birds of a minor, mundane paradise,
epiphanic only to an attentive eye,
as Mark says truth must be hidden
from those not in the know.

Glasswing Butterflies

Greta oto,
who do not wish to be left alone,
plunder dead Wood Nymphs,
of pheromones,
having none of their own.

A classic conundrum,
if ever there were one.
Tarted up in stolen perfumes,
how do they know to know one another,
in whatever sense you choose?

Great Egret at Moonset

On a November afternoon along Stewart's Run,
a Hiroshige landscape comes to life—
earth and grass crisp with cold and early snow,
bare trees stark on cold hills,
pale moon swollen in the western sky.
A late traveler for its kind,
the great white bird watches the stream,
and stops the day's decline.
Then, spreading vast wings, ascends,
laden with metaphors, into the closing day.

Anglewings

Butterflies cluster on fallen fruit,
sip an ooze of sweet decay
from split apples not swept away
by rain or human agency.

Carrion flies with flat, incessant buzz,
drink blood in Gilgamesh,
savor the stench of sacrifice
amid Mesopotamian mud.

Bees swarm to the honeyed light
of Dante's Mystic Rose,
gather nectar and pollen,
bread and wine for the ever-blessed.

Deep-deckled wings mimic dead leaves
around apples ruined by August sun.
Who has summoned these for us?
What saints declare themselves for us,
against our profane day?

April aquarelle

It's the usual April aquarelle,
magenta wash of redbuds,
rusty lace of maple,
pale chartreuse of new opened dogwood,
the same old thing, forever new.

Strange Communion

Day's field mirrors star streams—
clusters of ironweed,
constellations of asters,
a galaxy of goldenrod in slant September sun.

Starveling hornets, rag-winged honeybees,
spiders slow with egg sacs in morning chill—
a lightning scythe of fanged limb
reaps summer's worn surplus.

In wolfish orison
the mantis elevates these hapless hosts,
consumes them for her renewal.

Birds of Paradise

Are gaudy crows,
illuminated letters on the jungle's page,
so unlike angels,
those now familiar strangers—
too much in the public eye.

When did angels trade
argus-eyed primaries,
the green and roseate sunsets,
of parrots' wings

for whitewash?

Jumping Spider

Arachnid saltimbanque,
jewel-backed, black,
a swarm of eyes intense
above tiny fangs,
ready to challenge or retreat
before the brobdingnagian digit
descending from the sky—
a god's forefinger—
big enough to obliterate
any tiny invertebrate
too bold to favor
discretion over valor.

Grand Union Canal

Too still to be real
but for the blink of a yellow eye,
a heron waits for a meal
as evening settles
on a Little Venice,
too still for the greater one.

Chorus

Under the flat light of a mid-March sky clean of clouds,
a chorus, persisted through still bare trees
a querulous gabble
rising and fading on the warm edged breeze,
scores of ducks in colloquy, or so it seemed
until sight denied it.

Nepenthes

The pitchers dangle, puffed out, freckled rust and olive.
Their wet, bloodridged lips open around slippery throats,
A final horror for any stray invertebrate.
Nature's oubliette suspended from a leaf
Recalls Eden after the fall,
A recollection of jungle safe behind sweating glass.

Doves and Ivy

A clatter of wingtips one against another
made me see
rock doves busy among clusters
of wax-white berries on poison ivy.
Greedy for the pallid fruit,
they tumbled among whip limber spokes,
hovered on slate wings for a moment's purchase,
and a crop full of ivory beads.
Feathered trash gorging on fruit that could blister Achilles.

An echo of Eden,
or cold, organic irony?

The doves floated among the helixed branches,
wings iridescent in morning air,
indifferent to the question.

Manatees

Cruising in blue noon, the manatees snooze,
and dream of infinite vegetation,
oblivious, or so it seems,
to swarms of us agape at them.

Ravens in February

Birds—creatures of concupiscence,
carnality on the wing,
feathered frenzies of sensuality,
or so it's been said.
Two ravens flirt in cold morning gray,
call and cavort the way only they can,
snap-rolling clattering, half stalling
in aerobatic delight.

St. Vincent's

The pilgrims murmur along the walls,
obeisant at each station—
the old shoes, the well-used pipe,
lumpen peasants at a humble meal
a field lit by crows and sun—

They pause,
before the auto-icons
—the green eyes, the rusty beard,
halos of pigment radiant round the haggard face—
listen to exegetical impromptus
or formal excursions on the obvious,

enduring all to earn the cockleshell,
some for duty, others for love,
a few because some fool prescribed it.

The Basilica—Vicenza

A capsized copper hull
surmounts the mercantile temple,
Rome reborn in the Veneto.
Loggias where no kyries echoed
and no righteous scourge
disturbed the exchange.
Doves erupt beneath Palladio's formal orders,
fly from Doric to Ionic,
to undisciplined space
beyond the reach of architecture.

Road Show

As the U-Bahn rattles from the Volksoper
to the Allgemeines Krankenhaus,
stolid Austrians in fusty lodens,
women in oddly mannish hats,
varicosed men in lederhosen,
pretend to study the system map
while a couple in fashionable patchwork
gleefully grope each other to ecstasy,
to disturb the imperturbable
middle European bourgeoisie.
A vain search for aspersion
in the town Freud made famous
for repression and perversion.

Mysticism in Vienna

The tram stop at Wahringerstrasse
serves up the Volksoper,
a confection fit for merry widows.
In the Tibetan restaurant
across from this pastel panettone
the Dalai Lama serenes it from a poster,
rose-cheeked epicanthic children
bustle among the coffee tables,
while earnest Austrians debate the Buddha,
sip butter-tea among prayer flags,
their "Aufklarungs" ringing clear.

Via Dolorosa

Along the Kapuzinerberg's vertical way of woe
statuary stands in for piety—
the Passion, life-sized, a bit shabby,
caged against omnipresent swarms of tourists
or other legions,
the mocking, the scourging, the crowning with thorns,
the three falls, the nailing in, etcetera.
Beyond Golgotha, the Franziskischloss,
where beer and karaoke absolve pilgrims
sturdy enough to trudge the asphalted way
through managed beeches, oaks and pines,
well-mannered dwellings for ruder gods at bay.

Venice—Ghetto Nuovo

A long walk from the Rialto
on a November afternoon,
old stones, antique light,
a pastel courtyard,
shops like museums
for honey cakes, phylacteries, memories,
smoke and ashes,
perpetual loss and longing
carried on spiced or bitter wind.

St. Rupert's at the Dom

Beneath the dome
Blasmusik blares through bronze doors,
brass and drum earthing the aethereal.

In a courtyard smelling of horse manure and tourists,
severely dirndled old women distribute
coarsely salted bread and sprigs of grain.
Radiant in polyester cloth of gold,
the saint poses for fees.

Die Hexe

Christ dies everywhere in Salzburg,
his agony a street corner commonplace.
St. Sebastian suffers also,
smug putti tugging his darts.

The Other Side advertises too,
but nothing scaly this time,
just Lilith in black leather
smoking a cigarette on a rainy night
beneath the arches of Mozart's Wohnhaus,
outside the garden gate, of course,
waiting for a stray soul in search of art,
who, when he finally does turn up,
proves too cold and wet for any darker purpose.
So she turns a familiar trick when his back is turned,
leaving thin air and a black mouse,
to raise his hackles, if nothing else.

At the Proms

Across from the Royal Guild of Organists,
standees lounge along the wall.
From the broadcast van medusa to Queen's Gate,
they share evening papers, evening meals,
wait to occupy the balustrades
in the vast Victorian drum of the Albert Hall.

Informal tradition rigidly enforced
reserves places for these veterans
with memories of a matchless Mahler,
a Tchaikovsky mauled by a rude baton,
and officious ushers who ban food
to satisfy a brick-brained whim.

Inured to pains in legs and backs,
they assume yoga positions along the walls,
unlimber scores and opera glasses,
sit tailor fashion, piece a quilt,
initiate strangers into the guild
of those who suffer on art's behalf.

Gems

The Dutch once set diamonds on jet,
Sly modesty, that.

Now Dutch girls on bicycles
Flash past
Fashionable in black
From sweater to tights,
Displaying ivory skin, gold hair,
Sapphire eyes,
Promising dusky coral delights.

Limbo is Defunct

Pagan babies no longer dwell
In the easiest rooms in Hell.
Now that they are gone to glory,
What's the fate of Purgatory?

And they all moved away from me,

to somewhere or other
after I'd spawned a chimera
made them blink with wonder.
Did he say Marx had brothers?
Who is Marx?
They smiled,
and they all moved away from me
to some time, or other.

Hit the Road, Jack

Ray sang "Hit the road, Jack!"
and we did, with the best of intentions,
along a course of yellow brick,
divergent in a yellow wood,
or one dark with error,
with Maybellene, or Sal and Dean
down route 66 to Dead Man's Curve
to the sweet hereafter—
a long strange trip—
and always flirting with disaster.

At the Rock and Roll Mausoleum

In a bright and airy space,
they've got Jerry Garcia
or at least his guitars, encased
as in a shrine.
What little of Elvis Graceland could spare,
Moondog's dead microphones,
St. Hendrix's soiled green boots,
rainbow rags and glitter,
Robert Johnson no longer bedeviled,
no sympathy either for Old Mick,
Noli me tangere for all that energy
safely stuffed behind glass
like the Great Auk or any other Byrds.

Faith 'N' Janis

"Take another little piece o' my heart now, baby."
Sure thing, honey
But whose?
country cream and cotton candy
sunshine and lip gloss
cute, melting valentine confection
sweetie pie voice and clean blonde hair
straight from Nashville's dream machine
or
blood and night
glittering arc of Southern Comfort
Hair frozen wild in Fillmore strobes
sex and sweat
full tilt boogie
a voice that bleeds pain
to prove that popbeads ain't Pearl?

Mall Walkers

Have they been here all night?
corporeal only after hours?

Parchment flesh in ragbag polyesters,
shuffling or striding
pursuing alien banners,
fleeing the hiss of the following scythe.

In shoes like Spanish Boots,
huge on clay-pipe limbs
they circle the gloom of suspended commerce
along strict meanders of tile.

I had not thought life had undone so many.

1789

The new pagans met at Paris to resurrect the old,

willfully ignorant of the cold people
who ignored Aurelius,
who expected more artful strangulation in the arena,
and more inventive postures from the whores loitering
to sate priapic urges spurred by spilled blood,

and copied them religiously.

Northwest Ordinance

Mr. Jefferson's ordinance
set geometry against wilderness,
point and line against the forest,
reason against the meadow.

As if jink of lark,
amble of bison,
tumble of sweet water
in its meanders,
might be vanquished by axiom,
straitened by rule,
trammeled to a grid
by a red-haired philosopher king.

Antietam
September 17, 1862

The Cornfield

Miller's cornfield on the cusp of autumn
waiting for the steel,
for the harvest that stubbles the field,
leaves nothing standing on wet, rusty earth.
The grain garnered,
wasted,
heaped where ranks and files stood
a minute before,
an easy walk to the Dunker church
where no one studied havoc,
preferring plowshares to a red blade,
an easy walk
on any other day.

Bloody Lane

The sunken road rambles the line
between Roulette's place and Piper's farm,
hedged by split rail fences;
a water course for mild September rain,
wheelworn a yard below grade,
too shallow for a proper grave,
a makeshift dwelling for Abaddon,
to whom hundreds paid cold tribute.

Kittyhawk
December 17, 1903

Four times aloft,
the contraption and its bicycle makers
astonished the gulls unused to share
mastery of the wind. The air
sundered at most a minute
before gravity resumed dominion
over canvas, wood and wire.

Majorana Among the Carthusians 1938

(Presumed a suicide by drowning between Palermo and Naples, the nuclear physicist Ettore Majorana may instead have sought refuge in a monastery.)

Swift as starlight in my head,
numbers revealed dark angels
in every equation,
a most elegant deception—

Pascal's fiery night
lined the seams of his coat;
mine crowds my head
with corrupting radiance,
beyond the eye's prism.

No more numbers,
spidered on cigarette packs
discarded to sea or air
between Palermo and Napoli.

Soft rose, sweet sage,
resin-tanged rosemary
renew innocence within these walls.

Three days of black tokens, dear family,
no more than that.
Here, olive trees yield chrism to cure the soul
of a Lazarus, reborn, truth-tainted,
in a silent order.

Body Politic

A black fist, a map of Africa
green, red, black,
taut against breasts the color of their milk;
a skirt, that if cloth could conjure,
might summon Mother Africa
with green parrot's wings,
sunset violet over Mount Kenya,
and umber of slow Congo,
or cover some ample-hipped Lagos market woman
the color of richest earth,
not slim white thighs and blanched belly.

She hears the lilt of the Antilles,
bitter tunes of Babylon,
rapid fire abuse by thug poets
raging at the fish belly world,
and thinks an offer of her sex
to any man dark enough
to join her to a ghost coffle on Benin's coast,
to scourge the sun in her hair,
the sea in her eyes,
might redeem her skin's guilt
and teach her the meaning of "nigger."

Wheelbarrow

So much depends
on a bag of skin over numbered bones
in a land where earth yields
crops of stones,
and a mother rocks on her heels
and moans
beside the wheelbarrow and its awful load,
her meager repayment
of borrowed clay
so briefly lent.

Crochets

Women of an age more certain than our own
crocheted things:
doilies to preserve appearances,
tablecloths, shawls,
tiny shoes stiff with starch,
family histories in bastard lace,
a braille of the past.

Alla Danza Tedesca

Omens seldom introduce themselves.
Only later do we see and feel,
the wink and nudge of sly foretelling.
Adrowse on a winter afternoon
amid a warm drift of bedclothes,
I listened to a late Beethoven quartet
and heard a charming German dance,
a sober Teutonic frolic
defy the vast fugue's impending force.

When out of half sleep a couple sprang,
arms linked, familiar,
my parents in peasant costume
in antic refusal of six decades' ending,
of death's demarcation,
of pacemakers and other machines to simulate living.
Briefly they danced, then dissolved
before the tide of sleep and forgetting.

The Twilight of the Gods

They stood so tall, so long ago,
When they were young, and we had yet to be.
Then we began—
And they knew what we did not,
That's the way it is with gods—
The greatest risk is knowing
What they know before we should,
Or ever—if Eden is at risk.

But in time they taught us what they knew
So that in time we might be them.
We took for wisdom and mystery
What they knew only as what they had learned
From their own now departed
Who had stood so tall, so long ago
When they themselves were young and did not know.

Now they are old or gone, or going.
Young only in photographs
In black and white, or colors
That fade as they have—or are—
Once secret wisdom discarded, followed,
Made quaint with time and change—
Forgotten by those who did and did not know.

Then, Now

In a motel rumored to house whores and dealers
we learn lessons about the past.

that pictures slow time's depredation,
belie memory's redaction,
to make us faithful witnesses of our past.

that layers of fugitive dyes perish too,
bleached by light and glacial fires of oxidation.

that pink bouquets go to brittle flakes,
long white gloves become costume,
chestnut hair to ashy blonde.

that a dinner jacket recycles to rag paper,
blond hair goes to snow or melts entirely.

that some bonds creak but do not break,
become fast again on sight,
defy time and space, at least for now.

My Father's Slide Rule

Napier's bones
logging the rhythms
of rotating machinery,
coils and varnish,
copper and currents.
Reality approximated,
numbered, divided.

June 1954

A fleck of rust or disc of blood,
copper rivet fixed in an Ohio sky.
Summer's full burgeon below,
the slide from solstice to equinox just begun.
Mars just over the neighbor's roof
so close, so close,
and all the stories true,
canals we couldn't see but knew them full,
lyric crystal cities,
Martians too strange for dreams,
ruins too old for candles to count.
My father perched in our makeshift observatory.
The telescope, tripod and ladder,
neighbor kids lined up for a look at War's planet
after nine years of peace.

Sankt Valentin

Incongruous green in November gloom
a tuft of grass floods a mind with bright recall
of a then spring day
when a boy walked a path of gravel and clay
above a cold pond in wind still tainted by winter chill.

Now an old man, he sits in a train at Sankt Valentin
looking at the grass between the bahnhof's bricks,
dragged back from reverie, below a zinc and pewter sky,
rain falling on carloads of muddy sugar beets.
Then, through five decades redacted
the one lately dead has newly risen
to whistle him across an Ohio lawn
as the station recedes along the car.

Epiphany

Something other,
neither mote nor beam,
a catch in the light,
snares vision out of self,
sea changes us,
no more, no less;
before quotidian tides submerge us again.

Autumnal

By the ruined barracks of the old Ravenna arsenal,
moonlight, stained old ivory by a wafer of cloud,
lights spears of sumac, and a phalanx of cattails
into half-believed epiphany.

Through a night pregnant with mortality,
we drive towards dark mountains
on the road from Akron to Youngstown;
weeds, rust, broken concrete,
abandoned tollbooths,
ruins of the future,
distract us from the death to come,
deflect us from traducing the past by memory's fabrication
of a happy woman tilting a child to upside-down delight,
no possible relation to a thrall of pain in a glacial room,
aware only of morphine's brief mercy and meager sleep.

Olive Hill Cemetery

In that long Saturday between winter and spring,
the moon's truest month,
hawks hungry for one another
weave figures of fierce lechery below milky cirrus.

Beneath wiry grass and ancient roses,
delegations of the dead
obey the folly of the living,
divided—
black from white, from red,
cross from crucifix from Solomon's seal.

Among deer bones dry of marrow,
and the bleached dome of a turtle's shell,
lichens obscure the divisions,
granting perfect rest to warrior, slave and master,
bound in one skin of iodine on ivory, on old wounds.

Evening Song

At the close of my grandfather's ninety-ninth year,
crows caucused in our pine trees,
their evening colloquy
a nasal mutter in fading accents,
nuances of two tongues,
two worlds
blurred to one indistinctness.
In the lowering darkness
they shouldered one another,
shuddered stiff, sooty cloaks,
shook themselves free
of the last scraps of twilight.

Requiem for D.R.

You are the refutation of the lie
that the dead are better off for being so.

A puppet now to the rules of matter and memory,
incapable of surprise,
no arguments,
no fabric of wisdom or folly,
no jests.

Something other now,
estranged beyond knowing,
you trouble my days and nights
and make me want to be troubled
by you alive again.

Unspoken

As Scott's party neared Antarctic oblivion,
they thought another person trudged with them
beyond the edge of vision,
incorporeal, but there,
an unacknowledged fellow slogger.

We scrambled and panted up the rocks,
summer at its ripest all around,
a friend and her daughter far behind,
a widow once, now remarried to a good and funny man.
She knew, and we as well,
that someone else walked with us,
unspoken of by kind request,
vainly censored,
never banished past memory's edge.

Ministers of Grace

walk among us
unknown...unknowing
rare beyond measure
reveal themselves in simple moments,
plainly dressed.
The good, the blessed
bear their burden
share that burden
with us, for us
unaware of what it does
to us...for us,
beyond all measure
change us ever.

Gone

for LJK 1946-2004

To ashes, not embers,
cold remembrance,
shared pleasure,
common anguish—
death's sordid irony,
eternal denial of past love.

Apple/Heart

How did it taste, I wonder,
Passion's fruit
Plucked whole from me?

Was the blood enough,
Or did you savor too
My hope
Mingled in the scarlet streams?

Did you shrug or pause a moment
To puzzle at the core, at love's seed,
Now naked to your thoughtless look?

Ghost

With sad eyes and pensive lip—
she haunts my evening theater,
upstages a patchwork cast of clowns,
carelessly displays herself,
then scorns her gifts,
mocks the fool who thought them special,
shames herself with others,
calls herself whore,
not lover,
in a sordid exchange,
enforced and endured,
across the final chasm,
cold remembrance,
from ashes, not embers,
eternal denial,
rehearsed off schedule,
played for an audience
all too willing to forget, and disbelieve.

It's Always Something

Something or other,
Something up,
or rotten,
In Denmark or elsewhere.
something old, something new
There was just something about her,
Something in the way she moves me,
Something wicked this way comes,
always something.

Leaving Her

(after Celan)

Parting?
Yes, as one separates pages
of scripture.

A delicate perusal,
half-hesitant
among the chapters of her being.

To read her words,
the I, Thou, She of her
in love's private folio.

Libation

Each gesture, every syllable,
stamped with rude grace,
ruined by stuttering muscles,
she confronts the ranks
of chardonnay and zinfandel,
burgundy and muscatel.

A fractious marionette,
estranged
from quotidian ease of speech and motion,
she forces limbs and tongue
to fitful obedience,
the cost graven in eyes too profound
for her clownish amble.

Judas Tree

What merited the millstone—
treacherous kiss
bought with silver,
or black abyss
that beckoned after?
What fraught the blameless branch—
fruit of betrayal,
or freight of despair?

Miracle

Imagine Lazarus
grown accustomed to the grave,
to infinite certitude,
to cool darkness free from pain,
mutability forever abated.

Then the summons,
the raucous gasp of stale air,
the awakening
to change and chance
to hunger, to human hurt,
to dying again.

Together

for Carol, January 9, 2011

Together for a double score.
A rarity these days,
Or so I'm told.
It seems to me no time at all
Since we set out down the road to now
Amid that January's snow.
Marry you again?
Four times ten!

Acknowledgments

"Evening Song" *Weeping with Those Who Weep: Poems of Bereavement*, edited by Barbara Smith and Arline Thorn, 1998.

"Icon Russe" *Grab-a-Nickel*, Volume 43, number 6, Spring/Summer 2003

"Memento Mori" *DCSH Journal*, Issue 42

"Palimpsests" *Grab-a-Nickel*, Volume 13, number 1, Spring 1991

"Requiem for D.R." *Weeping with Those Who Weep: Poems of Bereavement*, edited by Barbara Smith and Arline Thorn, 1998

"Road Show" *Grab-a-Nickel*, Volume 43, number 6, Spring/Summer 2003

"St. Rupert's at the Dom" *Grab-a-Nickel*, Volume 43, number 6, Spring/Summer 2003

"St. Vincent's" *Grab-a-Nickel*, Volume 43, number 6, Spring/Summer 2003

"The Basilica---Vicenza" *Grab-a-Nickel*, Volume 43, number 6, Spring/Summer 2003

"The Devil at Isenheim" *Grab-a-Nickel*, Volume 43, number 6, Spring/Summer 2003

"Vermeer--The Art of Painting" *Grab-a-Nickel*, Volume 43, number 6, Spring/Summer 2003

Made in the USA
Columbia, SC
12 April 2018